Forty-four Ambitions for the Piano

Forty-four Ambitions for the Piano

Lola Haskins

Contemporary Poetry Series

Orlando: University of Central Florida Press

Library of Congress Cataloging-in-Publication Data

Haskins, Lola.
    Forty-four ambitions for the piano / Lola Haskins.
        p.   cm. — (Contemporary poetry series)
    ISBN 0-8130-1003-9 (alk. paper). — ISBN 0-8130-1023-3 (pbk. :
alk. paper)
    1. Piano—Poetry.   I. Title.   II. Series: Contemporary poetry
series (Orlando, Fla.)
    PS3558.A7238F67   1990
    811'.54—dc20   90-10876
                                                                              CIP

© 1990 Board of Regents of the State of Florida
♾ Printed in the U.S.A. on acid-free paper.

Acknowledgments

Some of the poems in this book have appeared or are scheduled to ap-
pear in the following magazines: *New York Quarterly*: "Accidentals" and
"Modulation"; *Perspectives of New Music*: " To Play Pianissimo,"
"Grace Notes," and "Staccato"; and *The Beloit Poetry Journal*: "Making
the Choice."
    "The Pianist Who Keeps a Loaded Gun on Her Piano" is reprinted
by permission of *The Quarterly*, © 1988 by Lola Haskins.
    "To Play Pianissimo" originally appeared in the chapbook *Across Her
Broad Lap Something Wonderful* (State Street, © 1989 by Lola Haskins).

*This book is respectfully dedicated to Carolyn Reaves,
who opened the doors of music and let me in.*

Contents

One

Sarabande.

To Play Pianissimo

Does not mean silence.
The absence of moon in the day sky
for example.

Does not mean barely to speak,
the way a child's whisper
makes only warm air
on his mother's right ear.

To play pianissimo
is to carry sweet words
to the old woman in the last dark row
who cannot hear anything else,
and to lay them across her lap like a shawl.

Staccato:

The woodpecker drums
about the tree
a rising spiral

until even the highest smallest leaves
cannot help themselves

but shiver, then turn wild
at his bald beak
his head of stopped fire.

Dropping into the Keys

How from height to the ivory water
the white bird falls.

How then through the rising air,
fish shines.

Accidentals

Driving Thirteenth Street, I have the sense
that something has moved since yesterday. The
avenues as usual count down to Main, yet when
I arrive at work, I find the turn has taken me
half a block to the north.
    In the elevator I push three instead of
four. I spend the day compensating, leaning
slightly to the right, to allow for the unexplained
weight on my left shoulder.
    When the news came we adjusted, says the
family of the man who will not come home tonight.
Yes, puts in his wife, we have schedules to keep.
Yet sometimes I slip and cook for four. And
sometimes, when I go to serve, I find the food
has gone, and all my pots are full of tears.

Octave

It is what happens
when you spread the feathers of one hand.

It is the shadow
the bell's deep swing casts
on the desert, the round sound
of Ishi's mouth.

It is the sun
and her sister moon, slow-dancing.

It is what returns
when you are most alone,
calling across some dark orange dawn
to the farthest rim of rock.

Grace Notes

Sometimes dance
Astaire's clean brush before he taps

Or beast
the appetite surging in a hunter's throat

Or flight
a sail catching its breath before
it exhales the wind.

Sometimes lethal
brakes screaming before a car blooms

Or lingering
the way a tongue tastes metal long after
the nail's rung home

but always clairvoyant.
They know the stranger I will meet,
the trip I will take over water,
like Astaire,
whose last dance blossomed into air.

Two

The Prodigy

He was born with the fingerpads of the blind.
By eight he could tell if someone
had been at the piano before him,
and how long before, and who.
Beginning *Für Elise* one November afternoon,
he burst into storms of tears
because his sister had banged
her tuneless anger the night before,
and he felt the bruises still on the keys.

He was born with the ears of a dog.
He could hear his mother's skin decay,
the soft give
as her cheeks sagged just barely more.
Sometimes his face would cloud
because the moan of needles becoming
earth seemed so incomparably sad.
Or brighten. He had heard
the sun come out on the beating feathers
of birds, miles away.

He was born with his life in his hands.
Toddling, he learned the little bells
of Grieg. Then he mastered Mozart's
speech, its ache of clean and brittle
song. Then he learned to follow Bach,
crossing water from calm to flood,
up and down the stepping-stones
of the keys. He would dream
of his piano as if it were flesh.
In a room with a strange instrument
he would walk by it once or twice,
brushing it as if by accident
with his leg, his sleeve.

Sasha

Horowitz, in response to a question from an interviewer, stated that he and his wife had, unfortunately, never had children. His wife, who was at his side, clutched his sleeve. Vladimir, she said. Have you forgotten Sasha?

The half-played piece flies off
the piano. The beginner scrambles
on the floor. Horowitz continues.
The pages fall like wings.

The beginner is surprised
to find all sharps canceled.
Horowitz has felt his fingers
vibrate, traveling the skin.

The piece comes to an end.
There is darkness. Sasha
curls under a bridge. The
beginner lifts his hands.

Musicians Debate Embellishment

Only liars dress the dead,
pulling frilly pants on lamb chops.

Call it respect,
choosing your maiden aunt's silk step-ins
for her last rendezvous.

Well then, it's a waste of time.
A clean hit's what you want,
not this swing and dribble.

But fouled balls keep a batter alive,
make the fans forget their cold seats.

Well, when you have an appointment,
don't you go?

Of course. But you take the interstate.
I choose the old roads through towns.
In a Quik-Stop in Provo a young woman
fingers her lipsticked cup. All her
possessions are piled around her.
Her eyes are green as an emperor's jade.

The Task of the Accompanist

For Kevin Sharpe

Dear friends start up the drive.
Ahead, the great house looms.
Sun, pale as the underside
of a woman's wrist, falls
from its windows.
                  Seeing this
their breaths yearn, their two
hearts lean as wind bends trees.
They link arms and walk slowly,
discussing how the roads
the Romans built have endured,
and the tiled baths, with their
blue and inlaid eyes of boys.

Why Performers Wear Black

Because there is no black flower.
Because they are brides.
So that their hands can reach out of earth.
Because this is not practice.

Because they have agreed
not to talk with their mouths.
Because they know that sound
carries best at night:

the dip of feeding oars,
the loons' tremolo cry,
a whisper muffled in a woman's
hair, on the far dark shore.

Three

Fortissimo

To play fortissimo
hold something back.

It is what the father does not say
that turns the son.

The fact that the summit cannot be seen
that drives the climber on.

Consider the graceless ones.
The painter who adds one more brush stroke.

The poet of least resistance
who writes past the end of his poem.

Pedalpoint

A mother's heatbeat to her foetus
which unfolds like a dark lily,

the exits that dream by
in a day's drive

like joints of track, that enter
through the footsoles.

I can't help it.
I've sustained this note so long

it's in my bone, slides
through the music like a boat through

locks, passing in the Panama night
from the one to the other sea.

True Legato

Perfect seamlessness between notes can be achieved only when the distance between them can be bridged without changing the position of the hand.

Lifting one foot, the other falls,
walking over grass where a child
sleeps, whose small stare closed
to dark. So these hundred years
become one more, and a boy's mother
touches his hair one day and sees
in his eyes that he is no longer
a child.
      And she reads the stone
which says: Waking to Angels,
and tries to trace the notes back
whose stems break in her hands.
Lost, she rocks the tattered score.
She does not know she sings.

Mordent

A mordent is a trick of light
in a black sky,

a dangerous illusion
that kills the farmer mending fence,

the boy scout in his tent,
says the German in jagged ink.

Au contraire, returns Debussy.
A mordent is suspended time, languid

as absinthe spreading in a glass.
Lifting it to his lips

a man believes he can live forever
in a room of women

of low and shimmering dress.
In the cypress swamp an egret spreads

its wings, which shiver
like the lashes of a dreaming boy.

The Rest

An unpainted sky crossed by branches.
The exact time it takes a bird of hands
to fly between trees.

The moment in sleep when a man stops
breathing. A loss, as of dream:
four small red horses that gallop away.

Arpeggiation

A combed chord.

    A mother pulls sun through her child's white curls.
    Or: Four AM. Towanda jerks a blurry pick
        through dreadlocks.

A broken chord.

    Shiny bits of glass that speak until you believe
      you could drink
        from the bottle they were.

A rope.

    A thousand feet hand over hand up Malham Cove.
      If you look down,
        you fall.

Glissando

To glide,
your thin edge
cutting eyelashes of ice.

My lowest
dear, quit your crying.
Use the cold.

Your blades
make their own marks
as you ride

and soon
your windy cheeks
exult. Glissando says:

I fly.

Adagio

The swing in the hips of a man
who's known the sea,

the dim roll and drag,
the black or turquoise water

on which he walks, on shore
or far from land.

There is the peace in him
of the bird

who begins her warble knowing
she has all day to sing.

Allegrissimo

A Chicago Romance

His words get away, so many balloons
flying into the snow.
A quick chase, and the girl's skirts whoosh

into night and high-rise lights
beckon over the star-tipped lake, and the
girl cools her forehead on the window

and looks across the table the boy's chosen
at this restaurant
that's the top of everything.

And here the piece ends.
She is so happy, there is absolutely nothing
she can say.

Ritardando

For months Gahagan gathered in
his heart

like chrysanthemums,
like onions that shine in jars.

And he leaned across the fence
and talked weather

Miss Kappleman recalls,
the day he took three guns

and loops of bullets
and went downtown.

Four

Technique

Rock your hand
as though gentling a jar
where dark-chopped fruits have slept
among the lemon peels.

My wrists turn easily in air,
yet when I bring them to the keys,
they stiffen. Of course.
Such freedom takes a life
of long and daily exercise

until finally
every muscle moves the hand
and your boat begins to slide
along the river
red with years of leaves.

Around a bend
there is a tin-roofed house
on algaed piers
in whose one room
a woman's wrist shines

as her hand moves across
the page. If you beached now
you could walk there in an hour.
But you will not,
having chosen to go by water.

Overtones

It's a function of how our instrument is made,
she says. Whoever touches a key, you or anyone,
sets its harmonics to vibrating.

Her white finger falls.
A sky swirling with cloud.
A girl sitting on the edge of her bed.
The mark her slip strap leaves on her shoulder.
The thin line

she rubs with her left hand
to make it vanish into her skin.
The words that shiver in her mouth
though she has not spoken them

though she will never speak them
because by now he is high over Nebraska
staring across a huge wing
at the last vestiges of cloud,
which swirl like swizzled gin,
and then become nothing at all.

Sight-reading

Halfway through you realize
you know this room,

you know this glass of low gold,
you know the light that falls

on his hair, you know the eyes
of the Pole, Stefan,

how they feel on the skin
under your dress. And

you know the dim hall, how
you two lean on opposite walls,

how the air between you burns.
And you know you have beaten

the same circle, to return
to the place,

here in a stranger's house where
it seems forever ago

your sudden hands first told you
you were lost.

The Uses of the Metronome

Before you get sea legs
    you place each foot like a drunk
      walking a line.

You are a darer of tightropes
    each clenched inch
      braced for a fall.

But when the windy second comes
    that, thinking nothing,
      you balance to the deck's tilt

then, oh then, the world is utterly blue,
    the white sail slaps sky,
      and you fly, you fly.

The Power of the Right Foot

The power of the right foot
to hum the past
when the hand's moved on

is a high charge, not for
mirroring the scream
of the woman who cannot forget

anything, nor for ruining
clean whites by washing them
with something red.

Oh the foot must never nod
asleep but listen,
each toe listening, deep

in the quick of its nail
for the moment
the bride in her stitched pearls

turns to her groom
and smiles,
and lifts her veil.

Pull Down / Release

Here the climb really ends. Pull down
on the black note,

release on the white. You're already
there, the wind sheens

around you, soon you will begin again.
You are an old woman, light

in her bones. You are the mother who
tells her daughter, go,

and feels her own body ebb, the way sand
vanishes down a hundred tiny holes

when the tide recedes. Week after awkward
week you fail. And why?

Because you still believe you can hold on.
Listen to your hands.

They are not as young as you.
They know.

Performance Anxiety

Here is my case.
Right now I have inside
little dark flowers,
glittery shreds of foil,
and on that nest
my bisabuela's boot, size two, with spurs.

Open it, you say.
But the blood hurries to my hands.
I am an animal halfway,
a sudden scurry of fur
transfixed by your high beams.

NOTE: *Bisabuela* in Spanish means great-grandmother.

Five

Some Members of the Chord Family

1. The Major

Every morning he waxes his moustache
with a tiny brush, finishing the ends
with a twirl between finger and thumb.
His mother never had to tell him
to sit up straight. Early on,
he taught himself to deploy food
accurately to his high mouth
without looking down, a musical
skill akin to finding one's bedroom
door, no matter how dark the room.
At thirty he devised a six-point
inspection scheme he has never
felt the need to change. Looking
into the mirror, he begins it now.

2. Minor, His Wife

They met at Fort Meade the summer
of forty-two. She dove into the
pool in her new green suit. A strap
broke. For a moment her white breasts
swung free.
          That night the Major sat
on the edge of his bed. She was
an advance on his map, a skirmish
to be won. Across the battlefield
of his dreams he moved his tanks,
his guns.
          Dry, her pale hair floated
around her face. Her eyes were
the changing shades of water.
In all their married life, he never
quite touched her.

3. Diminished, Their Daughter

Amid the Dulles rush she perches
on her case, with its remnants
of old destinations, hanging from
limp strings. Her father has not
seen her fresh-dyed hair, nor
the shaven moon above her ear
which bristles to her palm.
For this, she shrinks to go home.
Yet waiting, she is a quetzal
among crows, a flash of green
and crimson feathers. She has
arrived carefully early. There is
no chance she will miss her plane.

Modulation

Lone

At five, with tight French braids,
I paraded to the teacher's clapping hands.
But when Easter came,
I alone refused to be a duck.

lean

At fifteen three fast inches
stretched my spine. Minutely
I'd inspect each inch of flesh
through endless English, French,
and Art. To the assignment,
tell me who you are, I wrote:
"a pencil with pimples."

learn

At thirty I discovered on a page
the theme of wind and stone.
And in my darkened house
with its children sleeping
beyond the one lit lamp,
I lost my mirror's name.

Lone

And now at forty, having
fled California, I return.
I am a sharp-topped rock
off Point Reyes, the one
that makes a cave at low tide.
Every year I am less. One day
I will be air on your cheek,
a single grain of sand
over which each November
the black ducks will fly,
and the monarchs, with
their thousand paper wings.

NOTE: In music, major keys are denoted by capital letters — A means A major — and minor keys by lower case — a means a minor.

Fermata ⌢

Fermata the thin silk umbrella
that shelters the box

whose strings fall away.
Fermata the paper husk that falls

from the gift we can unroll
across the sky, though our dull

eyes cannot say how red moves
to orange, or yellow to blue.

Fermata the moon, the white
light that holds, the full woman,

who watches without impatience
her own blossoming.

Fermata the oil made of light
which continues past its frame.

The rest of Lepic is here,
on the gallery wall. Oh see,

he has taken a step outside.
He is in my heart now,

as long as I live, like the woman
he hunts in every Paris street,

who came to him like a dark wind
from the south, the woman, Fermata.

> *as Accent*

A horn behind you which says GO.

    *

The sudden focus
on an ivory bill high in a pine

when for an instant
you were sure of what you'd seen.

    *

Any sharp pain.

NOTE: The ivory-billed woodpecker has been nearly extinct for many years. Not within memory has there been any documented sighting of this bird in the United States.

> *as Diminuendo*

Can you feel the speaker's breath as he comes closer?
Is it warm?

If it is warm, is its warmth gentle or hungry?
Does your neck think he will stroke or bite?

Do his words fade because he is leaving you?
Is he backing sadly away,
or has he turned towards another town?

Do you think he is falling asleep?
Can you feel his hands loosen on the keys?

Can you see the threads of his dream?
Do they shimmer like fishing line?

Have you noticed that he has been losing his hair?
That he is turning bald as an angel?

Do you really believe this ends in silence?

Values

Half notes are youngsters who do not know
what they want.

Quarter notes do not know they do not know.

Sixteenths and thirty-seconds are babies
who only count for something

together—tickety tack tickety tack they say
in a big hurry.

Oh but the whole notes have settled down.
See how they

sink to the bottom, how across the measure lines
they sing like stones.

Six

Where Music Comes From

One performer shakes it from
his sleeve, like doves.
Another draws gold chain
from his fingertips. But

now come hands which claim
to saw the heart in two. We
hold our breaths. The high-heeled
heart gets up and struts away.

A new act climbs padlocked
into water. We yawn. He does
not rise. The houselights come
on, which burn the skin like sun.

Gymnopédie

after Eric Satie and Henri Matisse

A ring of naked boys
dancing against blue
has moved my ear
to the throat of a simple piano
whose keys are so white
I am afraid to touch them.

Ten Minutes, A Weather for Piano

after Webern, Variations *Opus 27*

Sehr Massig

The suddenly heavy sun
sends the leaves deep inside themselves.
Such intensity cannot last.
She comes out, stands behind him.
The first drop's a startle on the back
of his neck, the second a diamond
on her left hand. By the sixth,
the sun never was and all the leaves
are slickening with tears.

Sehr Schnell

She can't help herself.
The words spill fast but don't satisfy,
like drops on a lake.
How can there be enough
when you want to drown the docks,
flood the smug houses to collapse.

Ruhig Fliessend

Light tips the leaves
then shines in all the green world.
Together they lean on the rail.
Her wet skirt has married her thighs.
Through his shirt his shoulderblades
yearn, where his father pinched for wings.

Fugue

after Shostakovich,
Fuga *No. 8 in e, Opus 27*

Here is the yearn that sews her life,
its gold fur dress streaked dark
by touch like a camellia, that hurt bloom . . .

    And yet times in white she sings
    and her hem's proud and long
    and she wears on her wrist the moon's . . .

and it returns, says any thread can break
but this, water wishing to be sky
sighs up and falls, the yearn remains . . .

    the moon's corsage, tall camellia
    over water, that path of shine where
    fingers go blank as stones . . .

and it returns. Every time she shuts
her hands, she opens them to find it
there, the thread to sew her fur dress

    to her skin, white as night sea,
    the yearn dolphining through
    . . .

Intensive Care

The pianist Sigismond Thalberg acquired an attitude of self-control by smoking a Turkish pipe while practicing exercises, the length of the pipe calculated to keep him upright and motionless.

The old man breathes
through a tube, his
long trunk strapped
tight, to ensure
that nothing tears.
Only his fingers move,
scissoring the air
then folding once,
twice, and again,
to pull a crane
whose flight wastes
nothing, not even
the tiny snips of sky,
which scatter when dark

falls. Stars glisten
out the window. The
halls turn still.
The last clean wings
have flown
from Mr. Thalberg's hands.

Making the Choice

*How often when marriage is on the tapis and the happy
couple are discussing the question of ways and means will the
natural query arise, What about a piano?*
       John Brimsmead and Sons, advertisement, 1902

A piano to wear on her finger.
A piano like a bouquet of flowers,
babies' breath and daisies,
held behind the young man's back
as he stands at her door.
What about a piano, he murmurs, dear?

In the dim-lit store a Chickering
draws her eye. Herman stands behind.
His hands ache for her shoulders,
for the hidden knee that rises and
falls. Maud leans over the keys.
A breeze teases across her mouth

a soft brown strand. Her parted
lips grow moist. She can hardly
see in the bright whip of air.
She leans out, over the keys.
Suddenly, everything she thought
was fastened, comes undone.

Seven

The Pianist's Fear of Death

The moment a finger's down
the tone starts to decay.
And so for years you stay
your hand.
        The horn man knows
he can hold only so much air.
The violinist lives between
frog and tip.
        What makes you
think you're different?
          The
row of tiny graves that blur
into fog, the way you never
know what you call,
when you whistle in that yard.

Playing Hiroshima

There are no finer audiences in the world.
Andre Pogorelich, *in* Pianists Speak

Did you know the ones with colds wear surgical masks
so as to disturb no one?
They do.

Did you know their small hands lie folded in their laps
like boats?
They do.

Did you know they kneel kimonoed for etudes, as tea
cooled by a mother's breath?
They do.

Did you know that skin can fall like snow?
Softly . . . pianissimo?
They do.

The Pianist's Dream

I shoulder in a sweat-stained bag
messages from one world to another:
lavender letters enveloped in My Sin;
long white envelopes like coffins;
envelopes with windows, factual
as the chest hairs of undershirted men
that say that someone owes, debt
gathered by being alive,
debts gathered like trophies
by someone who couldn't stop;
cards that don't care who reads them:
Home tomorrow. Laura died last night.
The sun streams unbearably in.

I have opened a gate.
I am halfway up the walk.
Then from around the house
the dog screams. No. I do.
He leaps for the letters
that are in my hand, my hand.

The Pianist's Next Day

Someone else
walked from the wings last night

black tails
adangle like dead crows. I mourn now

that, desperate,
I turned to him. I wake the less

for putting on
the stranger's blasé eyes who bowed,

set his bench,
then embalmed, note perfect, each piece

I played.
See my knuckles whiten— the bald heads

of an audience
all in a row. Listen. The marks

on my face
are the burns of their applause.

The Pianist Who Keeps a Loaded Gun on Her Piano When She Practices

The children know not to knock.
Double-sexed, I use both hands.
I tease seriously. The notes
tantalize, approach explosion,
fall back. It is the brink
that thrills when the high
walker sets her pink foot
on the rope.
           The children know
I would shoot, but not at whom.
I am not certain I know myself,
only that this deep readying,
this fierce first step over
air, is worth dying for.

Glossary

Accidental. The sign indicating momentary departure from the key signature by the raising or lowering of a note by means of a sharp, flat, natural, etc.

Accompaniment. The term today (sometimes) implies the presence of a principal performer more or less subserviently supplied with a background by another performer. This is not the original use of the word, which carried no suggestion of subservience.

Adagio. At ease. Slow (not so slow as *largo* but slower than *andante*).

Allegrissimo. The superlative of *allegro*. Merry, i.e., quick, lively, bright.

Arpeggiation. A choral "spread," i.e., the notes heard one after the other from the bottom upwards, or sometimes from the top downwards.

Diminuendo. Diminishing, i.e, gradually getting quieter.

Fermata. A pause. A held note, the length at the pianist's discretion.

Fortissimo. Very loud.

Fugue. Contrapuntal composition for voices.

Glissando. From the French *glisser*, to slide. The drawing of a finger down or up a series of adjacent notes.

Grace notes. Ornaments in instrumental music, indicated in very small notation.

Legato. Bound together. Performance of music so that there is no perceptible pause between notes. The opposite of staccato. Indicated by a slur or curved line.

Modulation. The changing from one key to another in the course of a section of a composition by evolutionary musical means.

Mordent. From Italian *mordere*, to bite. Ornament shown by a sign over the note.

Overtone. Any note of a harmonic series except the fundamental.

Pedalpoint. A note sustained below changing harmonies.

Pianissimo. Instruction to play (very) softly.

Rest. (1) Musical silence. (2) Notation of absence of sound in a performer's part for a length of time corresponding to a given number of beats.

Ritardando. Holding back.

Staccato. Detached method of playing a note (shown by a dot over the note) so that it is shortened—and thus "detached" from its successor by being held for less than its full value.

Source: Michael Kennedy, *The Oxford Dictionary of Music*. (Oxford: Oxford University Press, 1985). By permission.

Lola Haskins has published extensively in literary magazines and has won a number of prizes for her poetry, among them the *New England Review/Breadloaf Quarterly*'s narrative poetry prize, *Southern Poetry Review*'s narrative prize, and the *New York Quarterly*'s Madeline Sadin award.

She has broadcast her work over BBC radio, London, and on NPR. Her symphony libretto, *Symphony for a Saint* (with composer John White), premiered in 1988. She has had two individual artist fellowships from the state of Florida, and in 1984 was an NEA fellow.

She has taught computer science at the University of Florida since 1979, and lives on a farm outside Gainesville, Florida, with her husband and children. *Forty-Four Ambitions for the Piano* is Ms. Haskins' fourth book.